THE KIDS' BOOK OF BOOK OF PUZZLES 1

Dr Gareth Moore is an Ace Puzzler, and author of lots of puzzle books. He created an online brain-training site called BrainedUp.com, and runs an online puzzle site called PuzzleMix.com. Gareth has a PhD from the University of Cambridge, where he taught machines to understand spoken English.

Revised paperback edition first published in 2017

First published in Great Britain in 2012 by Buster Books,
an imprint of Michael O'Mara Books Limited,
9 Lion Yard, Tremadoc Road, London SW4 7NQ

 www.mombooks.com/buster Buster Books @BusterBooks

The puzzles in this book were previously published in
*The Kids' Book of Puzzles, Kids' 10-Minute Brain Workout,
The Kids' Book of Hanjie* and *The Kids' Book Of Kakuro*

Introduction, puzzles and solutions by Dr Gareth Moore
Illustrations by John Bigwood and Nikalas Catlow

A CIP catalogue record for this book is available from the British Library.

ISBN: 978-1-78055-504-1

3 5 7 9 10 8 6 4

Papers used by Buster Books are natural, recyclable products made from
wood grown in sustainable forests. The manufacturing processes conform to
the environmental regulations of the country of origin.

Puzzles designed and typeset by Dr Gareth Moore
www.drgarethmoore.com

Layout designed by Barbara Ward

Printed and bound in March 2019 by CPI Group (UK) Ltd,
108 Beddington Lane, Croydon, CR0 4YY, United Kingdom

Introduction

The Kids' Book Of Puzzles 1 contains more than one hundred brain workouts that will maximize your mental powers!

Did you know that your brain has **WAY MORE** learning power than an adult's brain? As you get older, parts of your brain that you don't use regularly begin to fade away – just the same as the muscles in your body become weaker if you don't exercise.

This book is packed full of short puzzles that will help you train your brain. There are lots of different types of brainteasers for you to complete. By doing a wide range of mental activities you'll get to exercise different areas of your brain and keep your mental powers in tip-top condition. Try to do one or two puzzles a day and see if you can finish each puzzle in under ten minutes.

The Kids' Book Of Puzzles 1 will help improve your memory and concentration. Upgrading your thinking will improve your performance at school and help you feel better throughout the day whatever you're doing, whether it's playing sports, solving a problem or even just chatting. The more you use your brain, the cleverer you will become!

This book is a brilliant start to improving your brain, but there are also other things that you can do to help. Your brain is a part of your body so for it to be in top condition it is vital that you look after your body too:

1) Take regular physical exercise. This will get your blood pumping oxygen to your brain and you'll think more clearly.

2) Sleep well. Most people need at least eight hours sleep per night. Some need less and some need more. But if you don't get enough for you then your brain won't be able to function to its full potential.

3) Eat breakfast. A bowl of cereal or piece of toast in the morning will help your body wake up and will provide the energy your brain needs to function during the day.

4) Drink plenty of water. It's difficult to think clearly when you're dehydrated, so make sure that you keep yourself topped up with water throughout the day.

5) Eat a healthy, balanced diet. Foods that are especially good for your brain include fresh fruit and vegetables, eggs, lean meat and oily fish such as mackerel, salmon, trout and tuna (though avoid any of these foods if you are allergic to them).

As well as tackling the brain workouts in this book, you can invent your own mental challenges throughout the day. You could start from the moment you get up in the morning by eating your cereal with your other hand, and finish by learning a new word from a dictionary just before you go to sleep.

Tactical games such as chess, cards or dominoes can improve your concentration, reasoning and memory skills. Reading is very good for your brain as it helps you learn new words and phrases, improves your memory and helps you make sense of the world around you.

There are all sorts of things you can do to increase your brain powers, and you can start right now with *The Kids' Book Of Puzzles 1*.

Every puzzle in this book can be solved by thinking carefully about the problem in front of you. You should never need to guess in order to complete the workout. All you'll need to solve the puzzles in this book is a pencil – **AND YOUR BRAIN**! If you want to time youself, then a stopwatch or clock would be handy too. You can record how long it takes you to complete each brainteaser at the top of every puzzle page.

Don't be afraid to make notes or write on the pages – making notes can be a good tactic to help you keep track of your thoughts as you work on a puzzle.

Check your answers at the back of the book. If you're finding it difficult to complete an exercise, it is okay to take a quick peek at the answers. Even when you have seen the answer it can still be a challenge to work out how to get there.

Remember . . . you are training your brain, so it's the **THINKING** along the way that's important, not the answer itself!

To keep up with your increasing brain power, the puzzles get steadily harder as you progress through the book. It's best to start at the beginning and work your way through, because sometimes the earlier puzzles will give you hints and tips that will help you with the later puzzles.

Are you ready to take the first step towards improving your brain power? Then turn to **Puzzle 1**, and enjoy!

The answers are at the back of the book.

The Puzzles

Complete this sudoku puzzle by placing a number
from 1 to 6 in every square, but with no number
appearing more than once in each row, column
or marked two-by-three area.

	3		6	2	
		5	2	6	
			1		
		1			
	4	2	5		
	2	6		3	

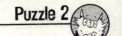

Find the fruits in the wordsearch square below.
They might be written forwards, backwards, up,
down or diagonally.

BANANA	LIME	PEAR
BLACKBERRY	MELON	PINEAPPLE
GRAPE	NECTARINE	RASPBERRY
KIWI	ORANGE	SATSUMA
LEMON	PEACH	STRAWBERRY

Y	P	M	L	Y	R	N	N	S	N
R	R	I	M	R	E	O	A	A	E
R	M	R	N	R	M	L	K	T	C
E	R	E	E	E	C	E	I	S	T
B	B	P	L	B	A	M	W	U	A
P	E	A	R	K	W	P	I	M	R
S	R	R	N	C	E	A	P	A	I
A	E	G	N	A	R	O	R	L	N
R	M	R	C	L	N	C	R	T	E
U	R	H	L	B	P	A	A	L	S

An anagram is a word that can be made by
rearranging the letters of another word.
For example, DOG is an anagram of GOD.

Unscramble the anagrams below to fill in the missing
words in these sentences. Each missing word is an
anagram of the word written in capital letters in the
same sentence.

A Her favourite fruits are LEMONS and *melons*

B He *drove* his car to DOVER.

C He rode a HORSE along the *shore*

D When I eat LIMES, I get a *smile* on my face.

E Take CARE when driving a *race* car.

F ROSE thorns can make your finger *sore*

G Every time you visit ROME, you find *more* to do.

H My uncle is a BORE who wears a purple *robe*

I At EASTER we'll drive a five-*seater* car.

J '*Finder* keepers,' she said to her FRIENDS.

K The men in the MANORS were held for *ransom*

L Witches have OPTIONS when mixing *potions*

M She ate it then STATED that it *tasted* funny!

N Wait in the *kitchen* for the sauce to THICKEN.

Find the following battleships
hidden within the grids:

1 × Cruiser
2 × Destroyer
2 × Submarine

Here are some clues to help you:

- Each row and column has a
  number next to it indicating how
  many ship segments are in that
  row or column.

- Ships cannot be placed diagonally.

- Ships cannot touch directly to the
  left, right, top or bottom (though
  they can touch diagonally).

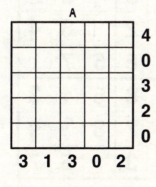

A

4
0
3
2
0

3 1 3 0 2

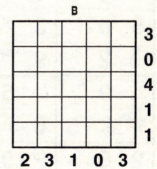

B

3
0
4
1
1

2 3 1 0 3

Complete this sudoku
puzzle by placing a
number from 1 to 9 in
every square, but with
no number appearing
more than once in each
row, column or marked
three-by-three area.

8	1	4	5	2	9	7	3	6
6	5	2	7	3	1	4	9	8
9	7	3	8	6	4	2	1	5
7	4	9	1	8	5	3	6	2
5	6	1	3	7	2	9	8	4
3	2	8	9	4	6	5	7	1
1	9	7	2	5	8	6	4	3
4	3	5	6	1	7	8	2	9
2	8	6	4	9	3	1	5	7

Fit all these animal noises into the crossword.
They can be written forwards or downwards.

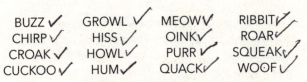

BUZZ ✓   GROWL ✓   MEOW ✓   RIBBIT ✓
CHIRP ✓   HISS ✓   OINK ✓   ROAR ✓
CROAK ✓   HOWL ✓   PURR ✓   SQUEAK ✓
CUCKOO ✓   HUM ✓   QUACK ✓   WOOF ✓

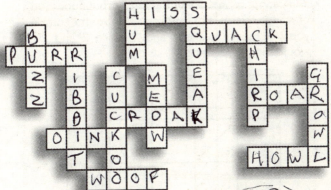

Five letters from the
alphabet aren't used in this
puzzle. What are they?

Complete this kakuro puzzle:

- Place any number from 1 to 9 in all the white squares.

- You must place the numbers so that each continuous run of white squares adds up to the total shown to the left or to the top of it (in the light-grey squares).

- You cannot repeat a number in any continuous run of white squares. For example, to make the total '4' you would have to use '1' and '3', since '2' and '2' would mean repeating '2'.

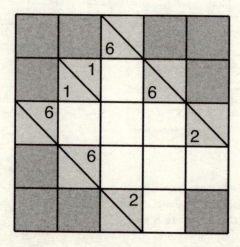

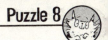

Complete these hashi puzzles by correctly connecting the wires to the terminals on the circuits:

- Between any pair of terminals, there can be either ONE wire, TWO wires or NO connection.

- Each terminal is numbered, telling you how many wires in total connect to it.

- All wires must connect directly vertically or horizontally, but not diagonally or with a bend.

- No two wires can cross one another.

- Wires cannot go over or under a terminal.

- The completed circuit connects in such a way that an electric current can reach every terminal by running through the wires.

Here's a solved puzzle to help you understand:

A

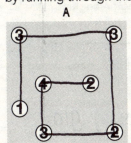

B

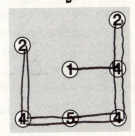

Look at these cartoon faces!

A How many faces are there in total? 49

B How many are either smiling or laughing? 15 smiling

C How many have one eye closed and one eye open? 12 of

D How many open eyes are there in total? 66 eyes

E Without counting, work out how many closed eyes there must be. 10

F How many are either wearing glasses or sticking out their tongue? 7 waring glasses

G How many are both wearing glasses and sticking out their tongue? 11

A How many circles are there? 6

B How many different sizes of circle are there? 4

C How many points are there where the lines of the circles cross?

D Where the circles overlap, new non-circular shapes are made (which do not overlap). If you wanted to colour each of these shapes a different colour, how many colours would you need?

E What is the least number of colours you would need to colour the non-circular shapes so that no shapes of the same colour touch at any point including their corners?

Complete this sudoku puzzle by placing a number
from 1 to 6 in every square, but with no number
appearing more than once in each row, column
or marked two-by-three area.

				2	**1**
		3	**6**		
		4	**1**		
2	**3**				

Shade the following squares in this grid:

- Shade squares containing even numbers. Even numbers are those in the 2-times table (2, 4, 6 and so on).

- Shade squares containing numbers that are both greater than 10 and less than 20.

- Shade squares containing numbers that are in the 3-times table (3, 6, 9 and so on).

- Shade squares containing numbers that are in the 5-times table (numbers in the 5-times table end in 0 or 5).

29	1	29	7	23	31	29	1	7	18
23	53	31	43	1	53	43	23	85	13
37	41	1	37	43	49	31	20	19	65
7	29	7	23	29	1	50	5	70	95
23	2	31	49	53	23	22	27	55	23
90	24	8	53	1	84	16	17	43	49
12	15	3	18	40	15	6	47	41	37
1	30	21	15	14	4	22	37	29	7
29	7	13	14	62	9	23	31	53	23
43	23	37	25	12	7	49	29	31	1

Complete these slitherlink puzzles by 'slithering' a line around each grid to link up some of the dots:

- The line must form one complete loop and use only horizontal and vertical lines to join the dots.

- The loop cannot cross or touch itself in any way.

- Each 'square' with a number in it must have precisely that many of its sides completed with a line between the dots. So a '1' has a line between the dots on one of its sides, but no lines on its other three sides.

- If there is no number in a square, it may have as many or as few sides completed as you need.

Here's a solved puzzle to help you understand:

1	3
3	1
1	3

A

3	1	3
3		3
3	1	3

B

1	3	2
0	3	2
1	3	2

C

3	2	0
2		1
2	3	1

Complete this kakuro puzzle:

- Place any number from 1 to 9 in all the white squares.
- You must place the numbers so that each continuous run of white squares adds up to the total shown to the left or to the top of it (in the light-grey squares).
- You cannot repeat a number in any continuous run of white squares. For example, to make the total '4' you would have to use '1' and '3', since '2' and '2' would mean repeating '2'.

The three pieces missing from this jigsaw are mixed up with some pieces from another jigsaw. Can you find the three pieces needed to go in the gaps?

There are 28 dominoes in a pack, each with two halves. Each half is either blank or has from one to six dots. No two dominoes are the same, and all possible combinations are found in a pack.

Which three dominoes are missing from this pack?

The missing dominoes are:

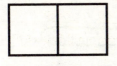

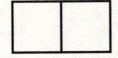

Using just three straight lines, divide the goldfish bowl into six areas, each area containing one fish and one bubble.

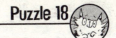

Complete this sudoku puzzle by placing a number
from 1 to 9 in every square, but with no number
appearing more than once in each row, column
or marked three-by-three area.

3	7	8	1	4	2	6	9	
6	9	5	3	2	8			7
4	2	1	9	7	8		3	
8	5	6	4				2	
	3		2		1		4	
	4				7	9	8	3
	1				3	2	6	
9			6					4
	6	7		1		3	5	9

Puzzle 19

Decipher this back-to-front story about computers and answer the questions below.

A In what year was the first computer invented?

B How much did ENIAC weigh?

C What was the original name of Charles Babbage's computer?

D In which country was ENIAC built?

E What non-electrical technology did Charles Babbage's machine use?

COMPUTERS

The first computer was invented by a British man called Charles Babbage in 1822. It didn't use electricity like modern machines, but instead had a large number of mechanical cogs. He called it a 'difference engine' because it could solve complex sums.

Although Babbage never finished building it, it was designed to work out tables of mathematical results. At the time, people employed to work out these tables of results were called 'computers', so the name became attached to Babbage's difference engine, and we still use the term today.

The first general-purpose and fully electronic computer was built in the United States. It was called ENIAC, and was finished in 1946. It was the size of a house and weighed 30 tons. It required as much power to run as an entire town.

These two pictures are almost identical. There are just ten differences between them – can you spot these?

Complete these kakuro puzzles:

- Place any number from 1 to 9 in all the white squares.

- You must place the numbers so that each continuous run of white squares adds up to the total shown to the left or to the top of it (in the light-grey squares).

- You cannot repeat a number in any continuous run of white squares. For example, to make the total '4' you would have to use '1' and '3', since '2' and '2' would mean repeating '2'.

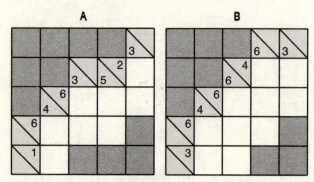

Find the action words in the wordsearch square below. They might be written forwards, backwards, up, down or diagonally.

BANG	EEYOW	POW	WHAM
BIFF	KABOOM	SMASH	WHIZ
BLAM	KACHOW	SNIKT	ZANG
BOP	KERSPLAT	THOK	ZAP
CRUNCH	KROOM	THWUNK	ZOWIE
	OOF	WAP	

Z	A	N	G	P	K	K	U	S	O	B
U	H	A	S	N	I	K	T	N	P	H
P	S	H	H	B	A	H	A	S	W	S
M	A	T	P	C	O	B	L	A	M	Y
O	M	Z	H	O	N	H	P	N	T	K
I	S	O	F	W	W	U	S	I	H	B
W	W	W	O	O	U	K	R	O	O	M
H	S	I	Y	B	M	N	E	C	K	O
A	H	E	I	O	A	Y	K	U	A	N
H	E	F	T	P	H	K	P	W	S	Y
E	F	O	I	E	W	H	I	Z	N	P

Complete this sudoku puzzle by placing a number from 1 to 6 in every square, but with no number appearing more than once in each row, column or marked two-by-three area.

1					6
	3				4
			2	5	
	6	1			
2				1	
4					5

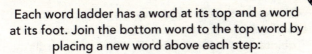

Each word ladder has a word at its top and a word at its foot. Join the bottom word to the top word by placing a new word above each step:

- Only one letter changes at each step, and it can change to any letter in the alphabet.

- Only words from the English dictionary can be used.

- For example, join MAT to COT like this: MAT, CAT, COT.

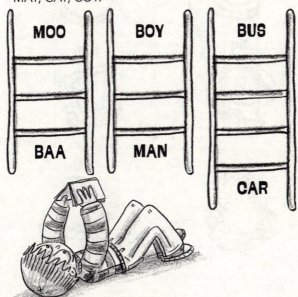

MOO

BAA

BOY

MAN

BUS

CAR

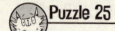

These coins are from Moneyville, where people spend quiddles (q) and quoddles (Q). There are 100 quiddles (100q) in a quoddle (1Q). There are six types of coin:

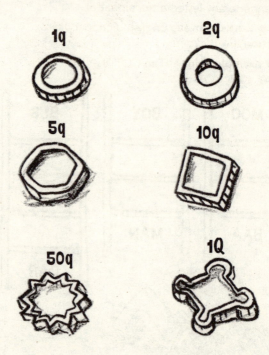

A If you had one of each coin, how many quiddles would you have in total?

B What is the least number of coins you would need to make up 1 quoddle without using the 1Q coin?

C If you bought something costing 87q using a 1Q coin, what would be the least number of coins you could receive your change in?

D You owe your friend 20 quiddles. What is the maximum number of coins you could pay him this money in if you were to give him no more than two of any coin size?

Spot these two pirates in the crowd.

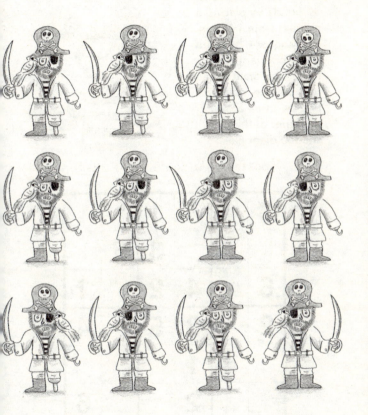

Complete this sudoku 'X' puzzle by placing a number from 1 to 6 in every square, but with no number appearing more than once in each row, column, marked two-by-three area, or on either of the two shaded diagonals.

3			1		
			3	6	
6		4	2		1
2		3	5		4
	4	1			
		2			6

Break the top-secret codes to reveal the
hidden messages.

Code Two is actually a hoax, designed to fool
an enemy if the message is intercepted. The real
message can be discovered by cracking Code Three,
but you will need to crack Codes One and Two first.

Code One
Each letter has been replaced by the letter that
comes two before it in the alphabet. So C is written
as A, D is written as B, and so on.

UCJJ BMLC ML BCAMBGLE RFGQ!

Code Two
Every other letter is false (the
second, fourth, sixth, etc.).

SKEMCLRIECTW MGAQP
YHZIMDSDRERNM INNM
GSALRADCE!N

Code Three
Take the false letters from
Code Two, then decipher the
secret message by applying
Code One.

Find the following battleships hidden within the grids:

1 × Cruiser ⬜⬜⬜   2 × Destroyer ⬜⬜ ⬜⬜
2 × Submarine ⬜ ⬜

Here are some clues to help you:

- Each row and column has a number next to it indicating how many ship segments are in that row or column.
- Ships cannot be placed diagonally.
- Ships cannot touch directly to the left, right, top or bottom (though they can touch diagonally).

A

```
        3
        1
        3
        0
        2
2 3 0 4 0
```

B

```
        3
        2
        0
        4
        0
2 1 3 0 3
```

C

```
        2
        1
        3
        0
        3
4 1 1 3 0
```

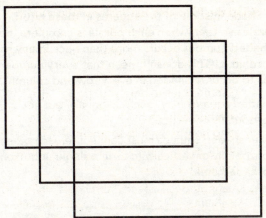

A How many rectangles are there? (Remember that squares are rectangles too.)

B How many points are there where the lines of the rectangles cross?

C How many different sizes of rectangle are there?

D Where the large rectangles overlap, new smaller shapes are made (which do not overlap). If you wanted to colour each of these new shapes a different colour, how many colours would you need?

Shade in some of the squares in these hitori puzzles so that, when each puzzle is complete, no unshaded number occurs more than once in any row or column. (This doesn't mean that every number has to occur unshaded in every row and column).

- Shaded squares may touch diagonally but not horizontally or vertically.

- All unshaded squares must connect to each other horizontally or vertically to form a single unbroken, unshaded area.

Here's a solved puzzle to help you understand:

4	2	5	1	5
5	3	1	2	4
2	1	2	4	3
5	3	4	1	1
3	4	4	5	2

A

2	1	3
3	3	3
3	2	1

B

2	1	1
1	3	1
3	2	3

Complete this sudoku puzzle by placing a number from 1 to 6 in every square, but with no number appearing more than once in each row, column or marked two-by-three area.

			5	6	
		4		3	1
2	4		1		
	1	2			

Complete these slitherlink puzzles by 'slithering' a line around each grid to link up some of the dots:

- The line must form one complete loop and use only horizontal and vertical lines to join the dots.
- The loop cannot cross or touch itself in any way.
- Each 'square' with a number in it must have precisely that many of its sides completed with a line between the dots. So a '1' has a line between the dots on one of its sides, but no lines on its other three sides.
- If there is no number in a square, it may have as many or as few sides completed as you need.

Here's a solved puzzle to help you understand:

```
1 | 3
3   1
1   3
```

A
```
3 2 3
2 3 2
2 2 2
```

B
```
3 2 2 1
3 1   2
2   3 3
3 2 0 1
```

C
```
3 2 0 0
2 2   1
3   3 3
3 1 2 2
```

Using just three straight lines, divide the web
into four areas, each area containing
one spider and two flies.

Clue: Only one line goes right the way across the web.
The other two lines go from the edge of the web to one of
the other lines.

Normal six-sided dice have spots on each face
to represent a number from 1 to 6:

Remember that you can
rotate dice so that the 2 and
the 3 could also look like this: ⟶

A How many spots are there in total on all sides
of a six-sided die?

On the dice below, some spots may have rubbed off
so you can't be sure which number each face shows:

B Which numbers could this face be?

C What is the minimum and the maximum possible
total of these three dice?

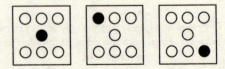

D What is the minimum and the maximum possible total of these three dice?

E What possible totals could you make using these three dice?

Spot these two pots of flowers in the garden.

Time ....

Complete this sudoku 'X' puzzle by placing a
number from 1 to 9 in every square, but with no
number appearing more than once in each row,
column, marked three-by-three area, or on
either of the two shaded diagonals.

	2		7	4	6		3	9
	4	3	2					6
7	9		5	1		4	8	2
6			9	2	5		7	1
	1	7	8		4	6	2	
3	5		6	7	1			8
1	6	8		5	7		9	4
4					2	8	5	
2	3		4	8	9		6	

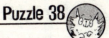
Complete each masyu puzzle by drawing a single
loop that passes through the centre of every black
or white circle:

- You can use only straight horizontal and vertical
  lines to draw the loop.

- The loop cannot enter any square more than once.

- At a BLACK circle, the loop must TURN then GO
  STRAIGHT on BOTH sides for at least one square.

- At a WHITE circle, the loop must GO STRAIGHT
  THROUGH then immediately TURN at ONE or
  BOTH of the squares on
  either side.

Here's a solved puzzle
to help you understand:

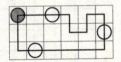

- In those squares that are not
  affected by a circle the loop
  can either go straight or turn.

- You do not have to use every
  empty square.

A
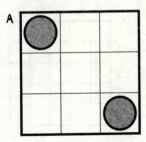

B
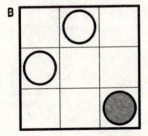

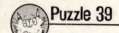

Shade squares in these hanjie puzzles to reveal the hidden images.

The clues at the edge of each row and column reveal in order (from the left or from the top), the number of consecutive shaded squares in that row or column.

For example, a clue '2, 2' would mean there are two shaded squares touching, followed by a gap of at least one empty square, and then two more shaded squares touching.

A

	1	1	5	3	1
1					
2					
5					
2					
1					

B

	1	3	5	3	1
1					
3					
5					
3					
1					

C

	1 1	1 2	1 3	1 2	1 1
1					
5					
1					
1, 1					
2, 2					

D

	2 2	2 1	1 1	2 1	2 2
2, 2					
2, 2					
1					
1, 1					
5					

Tip: Mark squares you know must be empty with a cross, 'x'. This will help you work out where the shaded squares go!

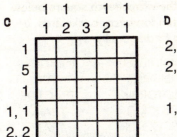

Find the vehicles in the wordsearch square below.
They might be written forwards, backwards, up,
down or diagonally.

AEROPLANE	MINIBUS	TANK
AMBULANCE	MOPED	TAXI
BICYCLE	MOTORBIKE	TRACTOR
BULLDOZER	ROCKET	TRAIN
CAR	SCOOTER	TRAM
COACH	SHIP	TRUCK
LORRY	STEAMROLLER	VAN

S	H	I	P	C	M	E	T	S	I	U
O	C	S	C	O	O	T	E	R	X	C
T	B	U	A	A	P	T	C	E	A	O
R	U	B	C	C	E	R	N	L	T	M
U	L	I	Y	H	D	A	A	C	R	C
C	L	N	R	C	L	I	L	Y	O	A
K	D	I	R	P	R	N	U	C	C	A
O	O	M	O	T	O	R	B	I	K	E
Z	Z	R	L	V	A	N	M	B	E	A
R	E	L	L	O	R	M	A	E	T	S
A	R	O	T	C	A	R	T	A	N	K

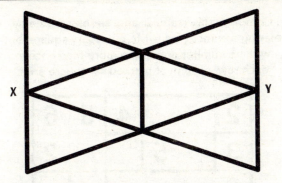

A How many triangles of all sizes are there?

B How many different sizes of triangle are there?

C What's the smallest total number of straight lines you could use to draw this diagram?

D Is it possible to draw this diagram without taking your pen off the paper and without going over any line more than once?

E If you drew a straight line from 'X' to 'Y', how many triangles of all sizes would there be?

Complete this irregular-area sudoku puzzle by placing a number from 1 to 6 in every square, but with no number appearing more than once in each row, column or marked six-square area.

2			4	5	6
3		5			2
4			2		3
6	2	4			5

 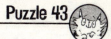
Complete these kakuro puzzles:

- Place any number from 1 to 9 in all the white squares.

- You must place the numbers so that each continuous run of white squares adds up to the total shown to the left or to the top of it (in the light-grey squares).

- You cannot repeat a number in any continuous run of white squares. For example, to make the total '4' you would have to use '1' and '3', since '2' and '2' would mean repeating '2'.

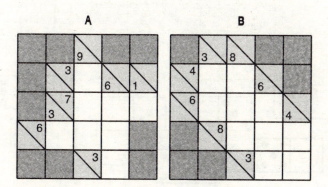

There are eight double-blank dominoes on the
opposite page. Use the dominoes below to
complete the domino chain:

- Dominoes can only touch one another when the
  number of spots on their touching ends match.

- You can only use the dominoes shown at the
  bottom of the page. You can only use each
  domino once.

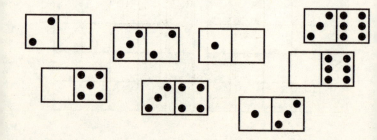

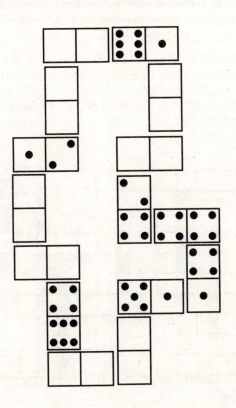

Fit all these vegetables into the crossword.
They can be written forwards or downwards.

BEANS   CELERY   ONION
BEETROOT   CORN   POTATO
BROCCOLI   COURGETTE   SPROUT
CABBAGE   CRESS   SWEDE
CARROT   LEEK   TURNIP

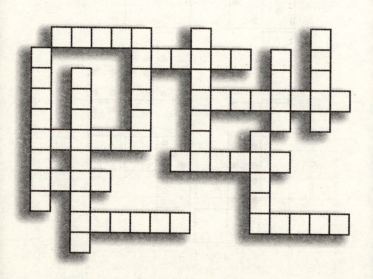

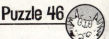

Solve these nurikabe puzzles by shading in some of their squares:

- Each number must end up as part of a separate group of that number of unshaded squares.
- Groups of unshaded squares cannot touch horizontally or vertically (though they can touch diagonally).
- Shaded squares cannot form a two-by-two block.
- Shaded squares must connect horizontally or vertically to form a single continuous area.

Correct

2		3	
3			

Incorrect

2			3
3			

These shaded squares do not all connect vertically or horizontally and there is a shaded two-by-two block.

A

1		1
		3

B

2		2

Complete this wordoku puzzle by placing one of the
following letters in every square, but with no letter
appearing more than once in each row, column or
marked two-by-three area:

N R K B A I

			N		
A			R		
	B				K
	K			I	
		R			B
			N		

Tip: Find the hidden word by
reading the letters in the shaded
squares from left to right and
top to bottom.

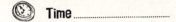

Each word ladder has a word at its top and a word at its foot. Join the bottom word to the top word by placing a new word above each step:

- Only one letter changes at each step, and it can change to any letter in the alphabet.
- Only words from the English dictionary can be used.
- For example, join MAT to COT like this: MAT, CAT, COT.

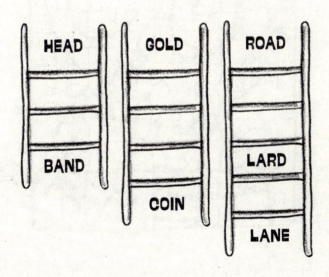

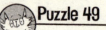

The four pieces missing from this jigsaw are mixed up with pieces from another jigsaw. Can you find the four pieces needed to go in the gaps?

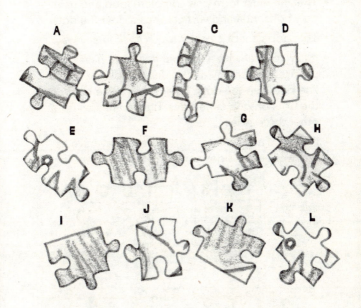

Complete these slitherlink puzzles by 'slithering' a line around each grid to link up some of the dots:

- The line must form one complete loop and use only horizontal and vertical lines to join the dots.
- The loop cannot cross or touch itself in any way.
- Each 'square' with a number in it must have precisely that many of its sides completed with a line between the dots. So a '1' has a line between the dots on one of its sides, but no lines on its other three sides.
- If there is no number in a square, it may have as many or as few sides completed as you need.

Here's a solved puzzle to help you understand:

```
1   3
3   1
1   3
```

A
```
1 0 0 0
3 2   0
1   2 1
2 1 2 3
```

B
```
2 1 1 2
1       2
1       3
3 3 2 3
```

C
```
2 2 3 3
1   2   2
1 2   1 3
3   2   3
  1 3 1 3
```

Shade in some of the squares in these hitori puzzles so that, when each puzzle is complete, no unshaded number occurs more than once in any row or column. (This doesn't mean that every number has to occur unshaded in every row and column).

- Shaded squares may touch diagonally but not horizontally or vertically.

- All unshaded squares must connect to each other horizontally or vertically to form a single unbroken, unshaded area.

A

3	1	2
2	3	1
2	1	1

Here's a solved puzzle to help you understand:

4	2	5	1	5
5	3	1	2	4
2	1	2	4	3
5	3	4	1	1
3	4	4	5	2

B

2	2	3
1	1	2
2	3	1

C

1	1	3
3	3	2
2	3	1

Time ....

Complete this sudoku 'X' puzzle by placing a
number from 1 to 9 in every square, but with no
number appearing more than once in each row,
column, marked three-by-three area, or on
either of the two shaded diagonals.

3		2	5	9		7		
9		8	7	2	3		4	5
	5					3		
			4		8			6
4	6		1		7		3	2
8			2		9			
		6					5	
5	9		3	8	2	1		7
		3		1	5	4		8

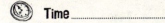
Find the following battleships hidden within the grids:

1 × Cruiser ▢▢▢   2 × Destroyer ▢▢   ▢▢
2 × Submarine ▢ ▢

Here are some clues to help you:

- Each row and column has a number next to it indicating how many ship segments are in that row or column.
- Ships cannot be placed diagonally.
- Ships cannot touch directly to the left, right, top or bottom (though they can touch diagonally).

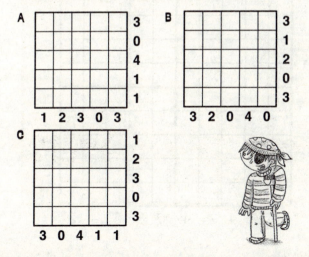

A

Rows: 3, 0, 4, 1, 1
Columns: 1, 2, 3, 0, 3

B

Rows: 3, 1, 2, 0, 3
Columns: 3, 2, 0, 4, 0

C

Rows: 1, 2, 3, 0, 3
Columns: 3, 0, 4, 1, 1

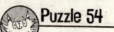

Shade squares in this hanjie puzzles to reveal
the hidden image.

The clues at the edge of each row and column reveal
in order (from the left or from the top), the number of
consecutive shaded squares in that row or column.

For example, a clue '2, 2' would mean there are two
shaded squares touching, followed by a gap of at
least one empty square, and then two more shaded
squares touching.

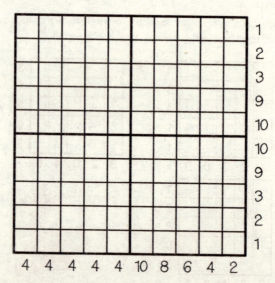

Complete this kakuro puzzle:

- Place any number from 1 to 9 in all the white squares.

- You must place the numbers so that each continuous run of white squares adds up to the total shown to the left or to the top of it (in the light-grey squares).

- You cannot repeat a number in any continuous run of white squares. For example, to make the total '4' you would have to use '1' and '3', since '2' and '2' would mean repeating '2'.

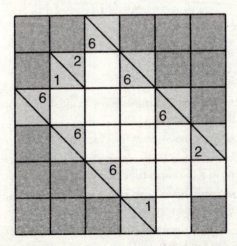

A How many stick figures have at least one arm up in the air?

B How many have both feet facing the same way?

C How many are both smiling and holding their arms in a U-shape that points either up or down?

D How many have both arms pointing down and one foot up in the air?

E How many have either their hands on their hips or are not smiling?

Break the top-secret codes to reveal the hidden
messages. It may help to look at things
back to front.

Code One

Each vowel (A, E, I, O, U) has been replaced with
the one that comes before it in the alphabet. For
example, A is written as U, E is written as A, U is
written as O, and so on.

**DED YIO HAUR UBIOT THA WIIDAN CUR?
ET 'WIID' NIT GI!**

Code Two

**EHT DLOG SI DEIRUB NI
EHT DRAY**

Code Three

This message has been
encrypted using Code Two.

Each letter has then been
replaced with the one that
comes before it in the
alphabet.

MTQ QNE QTNX DEHK!

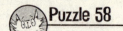

 Time ....

Complete this sudoku puzzle by placing a number from 1 to 9 in every square, but with no number appearing more than once in each row, column or marked three-by-three area.

2	4					8	9	1
	6	7			3			
		9			2		3	
				3	8	1	4	
			1		9			
	8	2	4	7				
	7		6			2		
			2			3	1	
9	2	4					6	7

These two pictures are almost identical, with the bottom one being a mirror image of the top. However there are also ten differences between them – can you spot these?

Complete these hashi puzzles by correctly connecting the wires to the terminals on the circuits:

- Between any pair of terminals, there can be either ONE wire, TWO wires or NO connection.
- Each terminal is numbered, telling you how many wires in total connect to it.
- All wires must connect directly vertically or horizontally, but not diagonally or with a bend.
- No two wires can cross one another.
- Wires cannot go over or under a terminal.
- The completed circuit connects in such a way that an electric current can reach every terminal by running through the wires.

Here's a solved puzzle to help you understand:

A | **B**

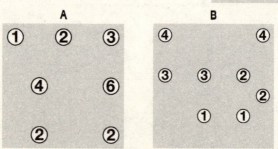

Complete this irregular-area sudoku puzzle by placing a number from 1 to 6 in every square, but with no number appearing more than once in each row, column or marked six-square area.

	4	3	1		
5					1
2	3		6		
		2		3	6
1					3
		1	4	2	

A How many triangles are there?

B Where the big shapes overlap, new smaller shapes are made (which do not overlap). If you wanted to colour each of these new shapes a different colour, how many colours would you need?

C What is the most sides that any polygon in this picture has? (A polygon is a shape made of straight lines that join up and don't cross over one another.)

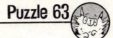

Complete this kakuro puzzle:

- Place any number from 1 to 9 in all the white squares.

- You must place the numbers so that each continuous run of white squares adds up to the total shown to the left or to the top of it (in the light-grey squares).

- You cannot repeat a number in any continuous run of white squares. For example, to make the total '4' you would have to use '1' and '3', since '2' and '2' would mean repeating '2'.

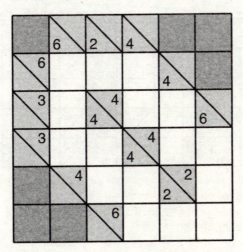

Complete these kakuro puzzles:

- Place any number from 1 to 9 in all the white squares.

- You must place the numbers so that each continuous run of white squares adds up to the total shown to the left or to the top of it (in the light-grey squares).

- You cannot repeat a number in any continuous run of white squares. For example, to make the total '4' you would have to use '1' and '3', since '2' and '2' would mean repeating '2'.

A

B

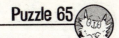

Shade the shapes correctly to reveal a picture:

- Shade shapes containing numbers that are in the 7-times table.

- Shade shapes containing numbers with the digit '2' in them (for example 2, 12, 20 etc.).

- Shade shapes containing numbers that are in both the 2-times table AND the 5-times table (for example 10 but not 2 or 5).

- Shade shapes containing numbers that are in the 3-times table (for example 3, 6, 9, 12 etc.).

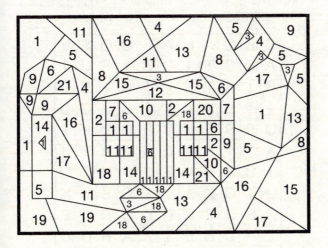

Find 'thank you' in many languages in the wordsearch square below. The words might be written forwards, backwards, up, down or diagonally. (You're not looking for the names of the languages.)

ARIGATO (Japanese)
DANKE (German)
DEKUJI (Czech)
DOH JE (Cantonese)
DZIEKUJE (Polish)
EFHARISTO (Greek)
GRACIAS (Spanish)
GRAZIE (Italian)

KIITOS (Finnish)
MERCI (French)
OBRIGADO (Portuguese)
SPASIBO (Russian)
TACK (Swedish)
TAKK (Norwegian)
TERIMA KASIH (Indonesian)
TODA (Hebrew)

O	R	O	A	H	A	F	O	O	S	E
A	D	O	T	I	C	S	I	S	U	I
R	I	A	T	S	P	T	A	I	E	O
I	T	E	N	A	I	I	C	J	O	U
G	B	R	S	K	C	R	U	D	K	I
A	T	I	K	A	E	K	A	A	I	J
T	B	A	R	M	E	G	I	H	O	U
O	T	G	K	I	I	T	O	S	F	K
Z	G	D	Z	R	R	D	O	H	J	E
Z	A	D	B	E	I	Z	A	R	G	D
S	R	O	A	T	T	J	T	H	E	P

Complete this wordoku puzzle by placing one of the
following letters in every square, but with no letter
appearing more than once in each row, column or
marked two-by-three area:

ZPLESU

P					
					U
	E		S	L	Z
L	P	E		U	
S					
					P

Find the hidden word by reading the letters in the
shaded squares from left to right and top to bottom.

These banknotes are from Moneyville, where
people count their fortunes in quidillions (Qd).
There are six types of banknote:

A If you had one of each banknote, how many
quidillions would you have?

B If you bought something that cost 95Qd by giving
the exact amount of money, what is the least
number of banknotes that
you could use to pay for it?

C I have two of each banknote.
How many banknotes will I
have left if I buy something
that costs 1365Qd?

D If you only use the
banknotes with numbers
that start with '5', what
is the least number of
banknotes you can use to
buy something that costs
1105Qd?

Complete each masyu puzzle by drawing a single loop that passes through the centre of every black or white circle:

- You can use only straight horizontal and vertical lines to draw the loop.
- The loop cannot enter any square more than once.
- At a BLACK circle, the loop must TURN then GO STRAIGHT on BOTH sides for at least one square.
- At a WHITE circle, the loop must GO STRAIGHT THROUGH then immediately TURN at ONE or BOTH of the squares on either side.
- In those squares that are not affected by a circle the loop can either go straight or turn.

Here's a solved puzzle to help you understand:

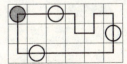

- You do not have to use every empty square.

A

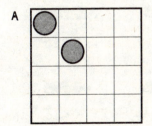

B

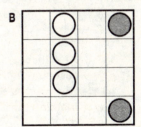

Spot these two monsters
in the crowd.

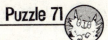

Solve these nurikabe puzzles by shading in
some of their squares:

- Each number must end up as part of a separate
  group of that number of unshaded squares.

- Whole groups of unshaded squares cannot touch
  horizontally or vertically (though they can touch
  diagonally).

- Shaded squares cannot form a two-by-two block.

- Shaded squares must connect horizontally or
  vertically to form a single continuous area.

CORRECT   INCORRECT

2		3	
3			

2			3
3			

These shaded squares
do not all connect
vertically or horizontally
and there is a shaded
two-by-two block.

A

2		
3		

B

1			3
	1		
	2		

Time ....

Complete this sudoku puzzle by placing a number
from 1 to 9 in every square, but with no number
appearing more than once in each row, column
or marked three-by-three area.

1		5				6	3		
	3							6	
	9	6	3	7					5
	6	4	2	5					
	7							5	
				8	3	4	2		
3				4	7	2	9		
	4							8	
		1	8			6			7

An anagram is a word that can be made by rearranging the letters of another word. For example, DOG is an anagram of GOD.

Unscramble the anagrams below to fill in the missing words in these sentences. Each missing word is an anagram of the word written in capital letters in the same sentence.

A 'I like your coloured MARKERS,' _____ Sam.

B He SECURED the boat and _____ the people.

C Display NOTICES in this _____ of the shop.

D You need good _____ to run on all TERRAINS.

E NAMELESS _____ are forever telephoning me.

F I have a _____ who is ORIENTAL.

G He TRIED hard to run, but he was too _____.

H She SAVES her money to buy ceramic _____.

I If you want to LISTEN it helps if you are _____.

J The _____ caught the CHEATER.

K On _____ we learnt about the DYNAMO.

L Everyone AGREES that _____ is messy.

M Which creepy-crawly is the NICEST _____?

N He saw a scary THING in the dark that _____.

Shade squares in this hanjie puzzle to reveal
the hidden image.

The clues at the edge of each row and column reveal
in order (from the left or from the top), the number of
consecutive shaded squares in that row or column.

For example, a clue '2, 2' would mean there are two
shaded squares touching, followed by a gap of at
least one empty square, and then two more shaded
squares touching.

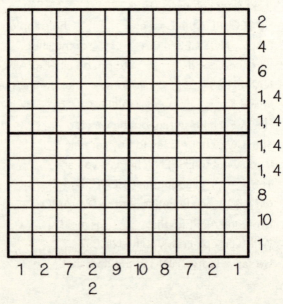

Using just four straight lines, divide the window into
four areas, each area containing one rocket, one
flying saucer and one star.

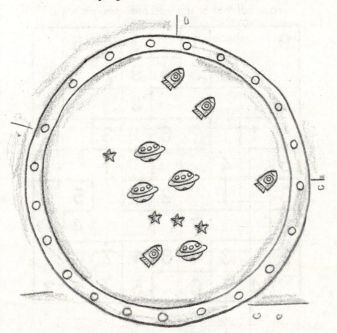

Clue: None of the lines go all the way from one side of the
window to the other. They all run only from the edge of the
circle to one of the other lines.

Complete this irregular-area sudoku puzzle by placing a number from 1 to 9 in every square, but with no number appearing more than once in each row, column or marked nine-square area.

9			1		3	4	6	
		6	5	4	9	2		8
	7				8			9
	1			6		3		2
6		4				1		7
3		1		2			5	
8			7				4	
2		3	4	8	1	7		
	4	7	6		5			3

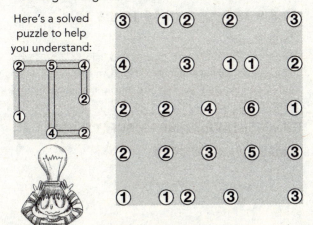

Complete this hashi puzzle by correctly connecting
the wires to the terminals on the circuit:

- Between any pair of terminals, there can be either
  ONE wire, TWO wires or NO connection.

- Each terminal is numbered, telling you how many
  wires in total connect to it.

- All wires must connect directly vertically or
  horizontally, but not diagonally or with a bend.

- No two wires can cross one another.

- Wires cannot go over or under a terminal.

- The completed circuit connects in such a way that
  an electric current can reach every terminal by
  running through the wires.

Here's a solved
puzzle to help
you understand:

Break the top-secret codes to
reveal the hidden messages.

Code One
Each pair of letters has been
swapped, for example **ABCDEFGH**
is written **BADCFEHG**.

ATEKISSXETSPAETSNAFDUOSRE

TSPONTRH

Code Two
Each letter has been replaced by a number
representing its position in the alphabet: **A=1**,

B=2, and so on up to **Z=26**.

20 8 9 19 9 19 3 15 18 18 5 3 20

Code Three
This message has been encrypted using Code Two
from puzzle 28, then Code One from puzzle 57. It has
then been flipped so that the whole message is back
to front.

RNAOKTUTAHRIBSABDIITCORFATTHSEU

MMEUSASRAUGOEIOYK

Find the following battleships hidden within the grid:

1 × Aircraft carrier

1 × Battleship   1 × Cruiser

2 × Destroyer

3 × Submarine

Here are some clues to help you:

- Each row and column has a number next to it indicating how many ship segments are in that row or column.
- Ships cannot be placed diagonally.
- Ships cannot touch directly to the left, right, top or bottom (though they can touch diagonally).

These two pictures are almost identical, with the bottom one being an upside-down image of the top. There are ten differences between them – can you spot these?

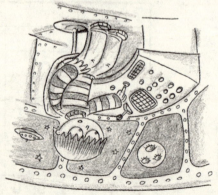

Complete this sudoku puzzle by placing a number
from 1 to 9 in every square, but with no number
appearing more than once in each row, column
or marked three-by-three area.

4	1		7					
			4	1				9
8		7	9		2			3
		4				2	6	1
	9						7	
6	2	8				5		
7			2		9	1		5
1				6	5			
					1		2	6

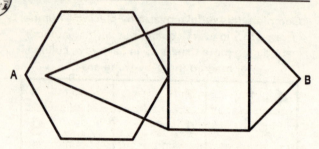

A How many triangles are there?

B How many quadrilaterals are there?
(Quadrilaterals are shapes with four sides. The
sides do not all have to be the same length.)

C How many hexagons are there? (Hexagons are
shapes with six sides. The sides do not all have to
be the same length.)

D Where the large shapes
overlap, new smaller shapes
are made (which do not
overlap). If you wanted to
colour each of these new
shapes a different colour,
how many colours would you
need?

E If you were to draw a line
from A to B how many
triangles would there then be?

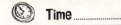

Complete these kakuro puzzles:

- Place any number from 1 to 9 in all the white squares.

- You must place the numbers so that each continuous run of white squares adds up to the total shown to the left or to the top of it (in the light-grey squares).

- You cannot repeat a number in any continuous run of white squares. For example, to make the total '4' you would have to use '1' and '3', since '2' and '2' would mean repeating '2'.

A

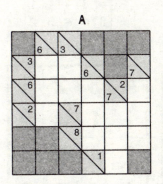

B

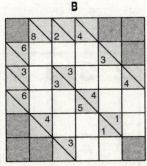

Shade in some of the squares in these hitori puzzles so that, when each puzzle is complete, no unshaded number occurs more than once in any row or column. (This doesn't mean that every number has to occur unshaded in every row and column).

- Shaded squares may touch diagonally but not horizontally or vertically.

- All unshaded squares must connect to each other horizontally or vertically to form a single unbroken, unshaded area.

Here's a solved puzzle to help you understand:

4	2	5	1	5
5	3	1	2	4
2	1	2	4	3
5	3	4	1	1
3	4	4	5	2

A

2	3	3	4
1	1	2	3
3	2	3	1
4	1	4	2

B

4	3	2	1
1	1	4	2
2	4	3	4
1	4	2	2

Time ....

Shade squares in this hanjie puzzle to reveal
the hidden image.

The clues at the edge of each row and column reveal
in order (from the left or from the top), the number of
consecutive shaded squares in that row or column.

For example, a clue '2, 2' would mean there are two
shaded squares touching, followed by a gap of at
least one empty square, and then two more shaded
squares touching.

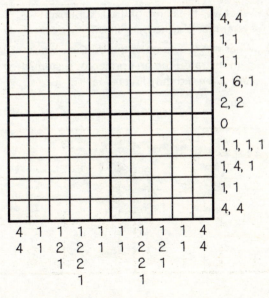

Decipher this muddled, back-to-front story about cinema and answer the questions below. Watch out, each pair of lines has been swapped, so that the second line comes before the first.

A In what decade was photography introduced?

B When were the first films with sound released?

C What was the name of the first public system for playing back films?

D What was the name of the brothers who demonstrated the first projector system? And when did they first reveal it?

photography in the 1830s,
Following the introduction of
playing a series of photographs
systems were developed for
the illusion that the picture was
in quick succession. This gave
in this way today. The first
moving, and cinema still works
reel of film with many pictures
public system to play back a
called the Kinetoscope, but it
on was revealed in 1893. It was
one person could watch the
was not very popular as only
the Lumière brothers
film at a time. In 1895, however,
Cinématographe projector
demonstrated their
cinema was born. Due to the
system in France, and modern
films were only a minute long.
lengths of film required, early
they were in black and white.
There was also no sound and
mainstream films in 1926, and in
Sound was first added to
produced. At this point colour
1934 the first colour films were
to make, and it was many
films were very expensive
widely available.
years before they were

Complete this sudoku puzzle by placing a number
from 1 to 9 in every square, but with no number
appearing more than once in each row, column
or marked three-by-three area.

	9	1			4	2	6	
	3		8	5				
	4	2	6					
2	6		5					
3		4		8			2	
		2			7	5		
		1	9	3				
	6	4		8				
5	2	8		3	1			

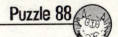

Complete these slitherlink puzzles by 'slithering' a line around each grid to link up some of the dots:

- The line must form one complete loop and use only horizontal and vertical lines to join the dots.
- The loop cannot cross or touch itself in any way.
- Each 'square' with a number in it must have precisely that many of its sides completed with a line between the dots. So a '1' has a line between the dots on one of its sides, but no lines on its other three sides.
- If there is no number in a square, it may have as many or as few sides completed as you need.

Here's a solved puzzle to help you understand:

```
1      3
  3    1
  1    3
```

A

```
2 1 1 3
1       3
1       2
2 2 3 3
```

B

```
3 2 2 3 3 3
3 2   1 2 1
3 1 1 1   3
2   2 1 1 2
3 2 3   3 3
2 2 2 1 2 2
```

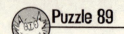

 Time ....

Shade squares in this hanjie puzzle to reveal
the hidden image.

The clues at the edge of each row and column reveal
in order (from the left or from the top), the number of
consecutive shaded squares in that row or column.

For example, a clue '2, 2' would mean there are two
shaded squares touching, followed by a gap of at
least one empty square, and then two more shaded
squares touching.

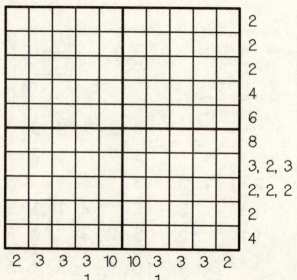

Row clues (top to bottom):
2
2
2
4
6
8
3, 2, 3
2, 2, 2
2
4

Column clues (left to right):
2 3 3 3 10 10 3 3 3 2
1   1

Find the cloud types below in the wordsearch square. They might be written forwards, backwards, up, down or diagonally.

ALTOCUMULUS
ALTOSTRATUS
CIRROCUMULUS
CIRROSTRATUS

CIRRUS
CUMULONIMBUS
NIMBOSTRATUS
STRATOCUMULUS

S	S	U	B	M	I	N	O	L	U	M	U	C	C
C	U	U	L	S	S	S	U	U	O	U	O	T	R
L	S	U	T	A	R	T	S	O	B	M	I	N	T
N	U	S	M	A	S	R	M	U	S	M	U	R	T
O	T	S	O	L	R	A	I	C	L	U	O	L	S
T	A	U	T	T	T	T	R	T	C	B	A	T	M
T	R	S	A	O	C	O	S	S	M	S	T	U	T
L	T	R	T	C	O	C	M	O	M	U	M	O	S
U	S	U	L	U	M	U	C	O	R	R	I	C	L
R	O	A	I	M	T	M	C	L	C	R	R	T	U
O	T	N	L	U	B	U	L	N	M	I	I	O	M
T	L	R	U	L	M	L	I	S	L	C	O	C	T
B	A	I	L	U	T	U	A	L	C	M	C	U	U
O	S	I	S	S	I	S	U	U	L	L	C	U	U

Shade squares in these hanjie puzzles to reveal
the hidden images.

The clues at the edge of each row and column reveal
in order (from the left or from the top), the number of
consecutive shaded squares in that row or column.

For example, a clue '2, 2' would mean there are two
shaded squares touching, followed by a gap of at
least one empty square, and then two more shaded
squares touching.

Tip: Mark squares you know must be
empty with a cross, 'x'. This will help you
work out where the shaded squares go!

A

	1	3	5	3	1
3					
5					
3					
1					
1					

Column clues:
2 1 2 2 2 2 2 2 1 2
2 3 3 2 2 2 2 3 3 2
(top: 1 1 ... 1 1)

Row clues:
4, 4
1, 1
2, 2
2, 2
0
2
2, 2, 2
3, 3
8
6

B

Complete this irregular-area sudoku puzzle by placing a number from 1 to 9 in every square, but with no number appearing more than once in each row, column or marked nine-square area.

5	3	2	9					1
	6	4	7		9	3	5	
					8		6	3
4					2			
6	4	9	1		2	5	3	7
		1						5
2	9		8					
	2	8	3		6	1	7	
1				3	8	2	9	

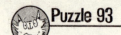
Break the top-secret codes to reveal the hidden messages. When you've cracked Code Two, you will reveal a question that can be answered by cracking Code Three.

Code One

Letters in this message have been coded to give numbers that represent their positions in the alphabet: A=1, B=2, and so on up to Z=26. However, these code numbers are not visible. Instead, the 'hidden' code numbers are the differences between the consecutive visible numbers. For example, the numbers '05 13' have a difference of 8 between them, and the eighth letter in the alphabet is 'H', so '05 13' is the code for 'H', and '05 13 04' is the code for 'HI'.

06 29 24 36 24 20 35 21 16

Code Two

This message has been coded so that every other letter, including the '?', is false (the first, third, fifth, etc.). These false letters, when read backwards, complete the message.

?WEHZYIDRIPDLTEHBEOCNOEWHWTIN

Code Three

Each pair of letters, including the '!', has been swapped around. For example ABCD is written BADC.

EBACSUI EW TSA UOSTATDNNII

GI NST IFLE!D

Look at these alarm clocks!

A How many clocks are there?

B How many are ringing?

C How many show 15 minutes past the hour?

D How many show 'quarter to' or 'o'clock'?

E How many are showing either 11:15 or 8:05?

F How many different times are there in total?

Time ....

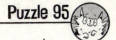

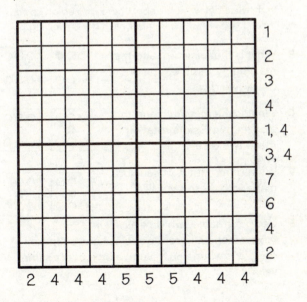

Shade squares in this hanjie puzzle to reveal
the hidden image.

The clues at the edge of each row and column reveal
in order (from the left or from the top), the number of
consecutive shaded squares in that row or column.

For example, a clue '2, 2' would mean there are two
shaded squares touching, followed by a gap of at
least one empty square, and then two more shaded
squares touching.

Row clues (top to bottom): 1, 2, 3, 4, 1, 4, 3, 4, 7, 6, 4, 2

Column clues (left to right): 2, 4, 4, 4, 5, 5, 5, 4, 4, 4

Normal six-sided dice have spots on each side to represent a number from 1 to 6:

Remember that you can rotate dice so that the 2 and the 3 could also look like this: ➔

A If you roll two six-sided dice one after the other, how many ways can you get a total of seven?

On the dice below, some spots have rubbed off so you can't be sure which number each die is showing:

B What is the minimum and the maximum possible total of these two dice

C What is the minimum and the maximum possible total of these two dice?

D What different totals can you make with these two dice?

E Using the same two dice as in **D**, how many different doubles can you make? (A double is when you have two dice of the same value.)

Shade squares in this hanjie puzzle to reveal
the hidden image.

The clues at the edge of each row and column reveal
in order (from the left or from the top), the number of
consecutive shaded squares in that row or column.

For example, a clue '2, 2' would mean there are two
shaded squares touching, followed by a gap of at
least one empty square, and then two more shaded
squares touching.

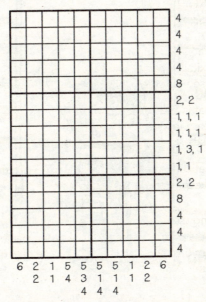

Each word ladder has a word at its top and a word at its foot. Join the bottom word to the top word by placing a new word above each step:

- Only one letter changes at each step, and it can change to any letter in the alphabet.

- Only words from the English dictionary can be used. For example, join MAT to COT like this: MAT, CAT, COT.

CAT

DOG

HIDE

FIND

LOOK

pigeon

moo

oink

SEES

This ladder contains clues to some of its steps.

Using just four straight lines, divide the field into
five areas, each area containing one tree,
one bush and one sheep.

Clue: Only one of the lines goes all the way from one side
of the field to the other. The other three lines run only from
the edge of the field to one of the other lines.

Time

Complete this sudoku puzzle by placing a number
from 1 to 9 in every square, but with no number
appearing more than once in each row, column
or marked three-by-three area.

3	9				6		4	1
				5				
7			1				5	2
2	6		8	7				
9				4				6
			9	1		3	4	
4	7				8			9
			2					
8	1		7				2	3

 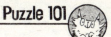
Complete this kakuro puzzle:

- Place any number from 1 to 9 in all the white squares.

- You must place the numbers so that each continuous run of white squares adds up to the total shown to the left or to the top of it (in the light-grey squares).

- You cannot repeat a number in any continuous run of white squares. For example, to make the total '4' you would have to use '1' and '3', since '2' and '2' would mean repeating '2'.

ANSWERS

5	3	4	6	2	1
4	1	5	2	6	3
2	6	3	1	5	4
6	5	1	3	4	2
3	4	2	5	1	6
1	2	6	4	3	5

A Her favourite fruits are LEMONS and MELONS.

B He DROVE his car to DOVER.

C He rode a HORSE along the SHORE.

D When I eat LIMES, I get a SMILE on my face.

E Take CARE when driving a RACE car.

F ROSE thorns can make your finger SORE!

G Every time you visit ROME, you find MORE to do.

H My uncle is a BORE who wears a purple ROBE.

I At EASTER we'll drive a five-SEATER car.

J 'FINDERS keepers,' she said to her FRIENDS.

K The men in the MANORS were held for RANSOM.

L Witches have OPTIONS when mixing POTIONS.

M She ate it then STATED that it TASTED funny!

N Wait in the KITCHEN for the sauce to THICKEN.

A
B

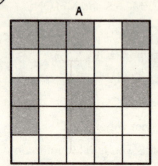
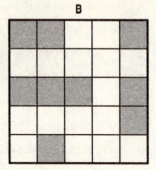

Puzzle 5

8	1	4	5	2	9	7	3	6
6	5	2	7	3	1	4	9	8
9	7	3	8	6	4	2	1	5
7	4	9	1	8	5	3	6	2
5	6	1	3	7	2	9	8	4
3	2	8	9	4	6	5	7	1
1	9	7	2	5	8	6	4	3
4	3	5	6	1	7	8	2	9
2	8	6	4	9	3	1	5	7

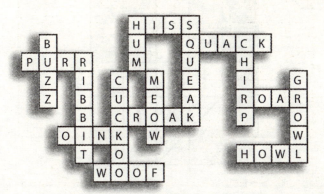

The five letters from the alphabet that aren't used in this puzzle are D, J, V, X and Y.

A

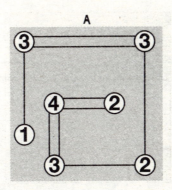

B

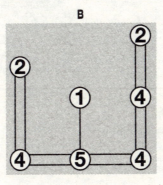

Puzzle 9

A 49 faces

B 27 faces

C 12 faces

D 66 eyes

E 32 eyes (49 faces each with 2 eyes, minus 66 eyes)

F 11 faces

G 0 faces

Puzzle 10

A 6 circles

B 4 different sizes

C 16 points

D 17 colours

E 4 colours

5	4	1	2	6	3
3	6	5	4	2	1
1	2	3	6	4	5
6	5	4	1	3	2
2	3	6	5	1	4
4	1	2	3	5	6

29	1	29	7	23	31	29	1	7	18
23	53	31	43	1	53	43	23	85	13
37	41	1	37	43	49	31	20	19	65
7	29	7	23	29	1	50	5	70	95
23	2	31	49	53	23	22	27	55	23
90	24	8	53	1	84	16	17	43	49
12	15	3	18	40	15	6	47	41	37
1	30	21	15	14	4	22	37	29	7
29	7	13	14	62	9	23	31	53	23
43	23	37	25	12	7	49	29	31	1

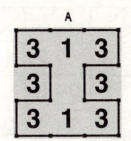

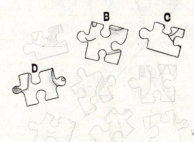

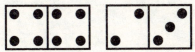

3	7	8	1	4	5	6	9	2
6	9	5	3	2	8	4	1	7
4	2	1	9	7	6	8	3	5
8	5	6	4	3	9	7	2	1
7	3	9	2	8	1	5	4	6
1	4	2	5	6	7	9	8	3
5	1	4	7	9	3	2	6	8
9	8	3	6	5	2	1	7	4
2	6	7	8	1	4	3	5	9

Puzzle 19

A The first computer was invented in 1822.

B ENIAC weighed 30 tons.

C Charles Babbage originally called his computer a 'difference engine'.

D ENIAC was built in the United States.

E Babbage's machine used mechanical cogs.

A

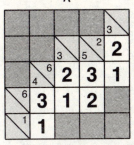

B

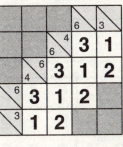

Z	A	N	G	P	K	K	U	S	O	B
U	H	A	S	N	I	K	T	N	P	H
P	S	H	H	B	A	H	A	S	W	S
M	A	T	P	C	O	B	L	A	M	Y
O	M	Z	H	O	N	H	P	N	T	K
I	S	O	F	W	W	U	S	I	H	B
W	W	W	O	O	U	K	R	O	O	M
H	S	I	Y	B	M	N	E	C	K	O
A	H	E	I	O	A	Y	K	U	A	N
H	E	F	T	P	H	K	P	W	S	Y
E	F	O	I	E	W	H	I	Z	N	P

1	2	5	4	3	6
5	3	6	1	2	4
6	4	3	2	5	1
3	6	1	5	4	2
2	5	4	6	1	3
4	1	2	3	6	5

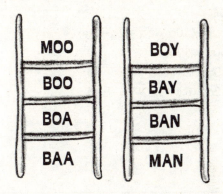

MOO
BOO
BOA
BAA

BOY
BAY
BAN
MAN

Can you find
any alternative
solutions?

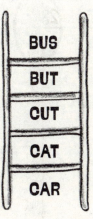

BUS
BUT
CUT
CAT
CAR

Puzzle 25

- **A** 168 quiddles
  (100q + 50q + 10q + 5q + 2q + 1q)
- **B** 2 coins (50q + 50q)
- **C** 3 coins (10q + 2q + 1q)
- **D** 5 coins (10q + 5q + 2q + 2q + 1q)

Puzzle 26

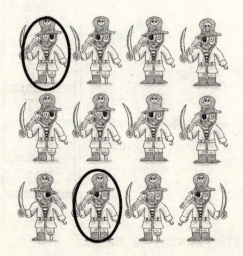

3	2	6	1	4	5
4	1	5	3	6	2
6	5	4	2	3	1
2	6	3	5	1	4
5	4	1	6	2	3
1	3	2	4	5	6

Code One

WELL DONE ON DECODING THIS!

Code Two

SECRET MAP HIDDEN IN GARDEN

Code Three

MONKEY IS ABOUT TO POUNCE!

Puzzle 29

A

B

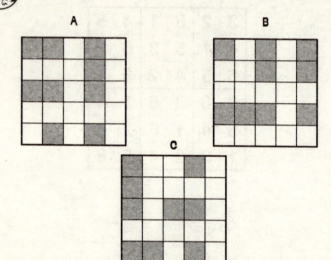

C

Puzzle 30

A 8 rectangles

B 6 points

C 4 different sizes

D 7 colours

A

2	1	3
3	3	3
3	2	1

B

2	1	1
1	3	1
3	2	3

4	3	1	6	2	5
1	2	3	5	6	4
6	5	4	2	3	1
2	4	6	1	5	3
5	1	2	3	4	6
3	6	5	4	1	2

A

3	2	3
2	3	2
2	2	2

B

3	2	2	1
3	1		2
2		3	3
3	2	0	1

C

3	2	0	0
2	2		1
3		3	3
3	1	2	2

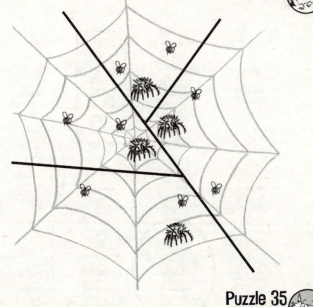

A 21 spots

B 2, 3, 4, 5, 6

C The minimum total is 5
The maximum total is 17

D The minimum total is 7
The maximum total is 15

E 10, 12, 14, 16

8	2	1	7	4	6	5	3	9
5	4	3	2	9	8	7	1	6
7	9	6	5	1	3	4	8	2
6	8	4	9	2	5	3	7	1
9	1	7	8	3	4	6	2	5
3	5	2	6	7	1	9	4	8
1	6	8	3	5	7	2	9	4
4	7	9	1	6	2	8	5	3
2	3	5	4	8	9	1	6	7

A

B

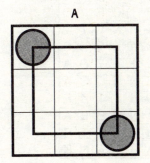
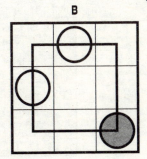

A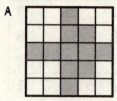

B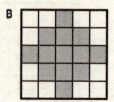

C

D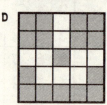

Puzzle 40

A 8 triangles

B 2 sizes

C 7 straight lines

D Yes

E 18 triangles

2	1	3	4	5	6
3	6	5	1	4	2
5	4	2	6	3	1
1	3	6	5	2	4
4	5	1	2	6	3
6	2	4	3	1	5

A

B

Puzzle 44

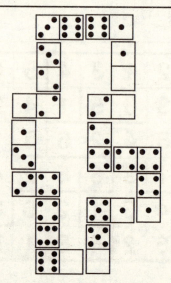

A

B

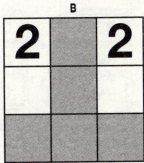

Puzzle 47

K	I	N	B	R	A
A	N	K	R	B	I
R	B	A	I	K	N
N	K	B	A	I	R
I	A	R	K	N	B
B	R	I	N	A	K

The hidden word is BRAIN.

Puzzle 48

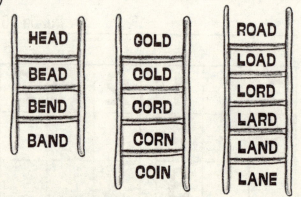

HEAD	GOLD	ROAD
BEAD	COLD	LOAD
BEND	CORD	LORD
BAND	CORN	LARD
	COIN	LAND
		LANE

Can you find any alternative solutions?

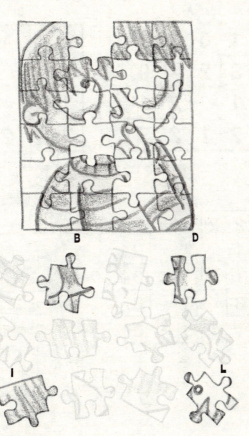

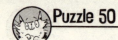

A

1	0	0	0
3	2		0
1		2	1
2	1	2	3

B

2	1	1	2
1			2
1			3
3	3	2	3

C

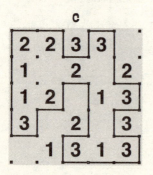

2	2	3	3	
1		2		2
1	2		1	3
3		2		3
	1	3	1	3

A

3	1	2
2	3	1
2	1	1

B

2	2	3
1	1	2
2	3	1

C

1	1	3
3	3	2
2	3	1

3	4	2	5	9	6	7	8	1
9	1	8	7	2	3	6	4	5
6	5	7	8	4	1	3	2	9
2	7	5	4	3	8	9	1	6
4	6	9	1	5	7	8	3	2
8	3	1	2	6	9	5	7	4
1	8	6	9	7	4	2	5	3
5	9	4	3	8	2	1	6	7
7	2	3	6	1	5	4	9	8

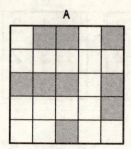

A

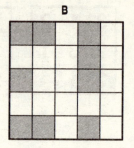

B

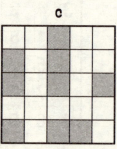

C

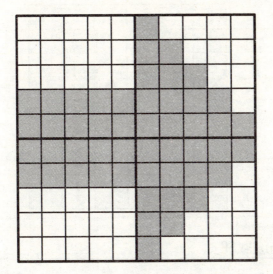

		6			
	2	**2**	6		
6	**1**	**3**	**2**	6	
	6	**1**	**3**	**2**	2
		6	**1**	**3**	**2**
			1	**1**	

A   12 stick figures

B   18 stick figures

C   6 stick figures

D   4 stick figures

E   16 stick figures

Code One

DID YOU HEAR ABOUT THE WOODEN CAR?

IT 'WOOD' NOT GO!

Code Two

THE GOLD IS BURIED IN THE YARD

Code Three

RUN FOR YOUR LIFE!

2	4	3	7	6	5	8	9	1
8	6	7	9	1	3	4	2	5
5	1	9	8	4	2	7	3	6
7	9	6	5	3	8	1	4	2
4	3	5	1	2	9	6	7	8
1	8	2	4	7	6	9	5	3
3	7	1	6	5	4	2	8	9
6	5	8	2	9	7	3	1	4
9	2	4	3	8	1	5	6	7

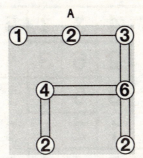

A

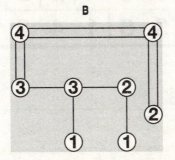

B

6	4	3	1	5	2
5	2	6	3	4	1
2	3	5	6	1	4
4	1	2	5	3	6
1	5	4	2	6	3
3	6	1	4	2	5

A 5 triangles

B 15 colours

C 17 sides

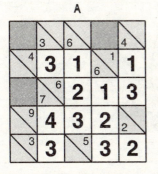

A

B

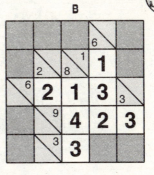

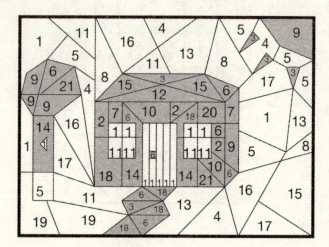

O	R	O	A	H	A	F	O	O	S	E
A	D	O	T	I	C	S	I	S	U	I
R	I	A	T	S	P	T	A	I	E	O
I	T	E	N	A	I	I	C	J	O	U
G	B	R	S	K	C	R	U	D	K	I
A	T	I	K	A	E	K	A	A	I	J
T	B	A	R	M	E	G	I	H	O	U
O	T	G	K	I	I	T	O	S	F	K
Z	G	D	Z	R	R	D	O	H	J	E
Z	A	D	B	E	I	Z	A	R	G	D
S	R	O	A	T	T	J	T	H	E	P

P	L	Z	U	S	E
Z	S	L	E	P	U
U	E	P	S	L	Z
L	P	E	Z	U	S
S	Z	U	P	E	L
E	U	S	L	Z	P

The hidden
word is
PUZZLES.

Puzzle 68

A 685Qd

B 4 banknotes
(50Qd + 20Qd + 20Qd + 5Qd)

C 1 banknote (5Qd)

D 5 banknotes
(500Qd + 500Qd + 50Qd + 50Qd + 5Qd

Puzzle 69

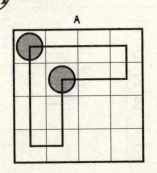

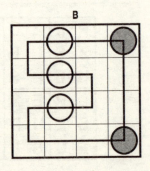

A

2		
3		

B

1			3
	1		
	2		

1	8	5	4	9	6	3	7	2
7	3	2	5	1	8	9	6	4
4	9	6	3	7	2	8	1	5
8	6	4	2	5	1	7	3	9
2	7	3	9	6	4	1	5	8
5	1	9	7	8	3	4	2	6
3	5	8	6	4	7	2	9	1
6	4	7	1	2	9	5	8	3
9	2	1	8	3	5	6	4	7

A 'I like your coloured MARKERS,' REMARKS Sam.

B He SECURED the boat and RESCUED the people.

C Display NOTICES in this SECTION of the shop.

D You need good TRAINERS to run on all TERRAINS.

E NAMELESS SALESMEN are forever telephoning me.

F I have a RELATION who is ORIENTAL.

G He TRIED hard to run, but he was too TIRED.

H She SAVES her money to buy ceramic VASES.

I If you want to LISTEN it helps if you are SILENT.

J The TEACHER caught the CHEATER.

K On MONDAY we learnt about the DYNAMO.

L Everyone AGREES that GREASE is messy.

M Which creepy-crawly is the NICEST INSECT?

N He saw a scary THING in the dark that NIGHT.

Puzzle 74

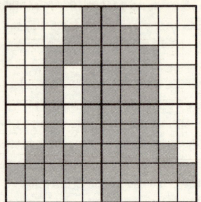

Puzzle 75

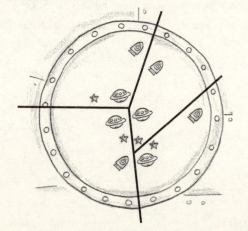

9	8	2	1	7	3	4	6	5
7	3	6	5	4	9	2	1	8
4	7	5	2	1	8	6	3	9
5	1	8	9	6	4	3	7	2
6	9	4	3	5	2	1	8	7
3	6	1	8	2	7	9	5	4
8	2	9	7	3	6	5	4	1
2	5	3	4	8	1	7	9	6
1	4	7	6	9	5	8	2	3

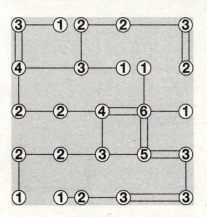

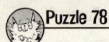

Code One

TAKE SIX STEPS EAST AND FOUR STEPS NORTH

Code Two

THIS IS CORRECT

Code Three

YOU ARE A MASTER CODE BREAKER

Puzzle 79

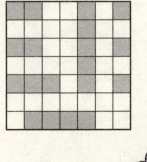

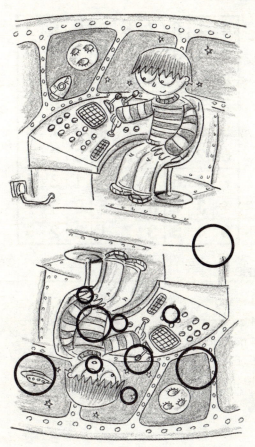

Puzzle 81

4	1	9	7	8	3	6	5	2
2	5	3	4	1	6	7	8	9
8	6	7	9	5	2	4	1	3
3	7	4	5	9	8	2	6	1
5	9	1	6	2	4	3	7	8
6	2	8	1	3	7	5	9	4
7	8	6	2	4	9	1	3	5
1	3	2	8	6	5	9	4	7
9	4	5	3	7	1	8	2	6

Puzzle 82

A 4 triangles

B 4 quadrilaterals

C 4 hexagons

D 6 colours

E 10 triangles

A

	6	3			
3	**1**	**2**	6		7
6	**3**	**1**	**2**	2 / 7	**2**
2	**2**	7	**1**	**2**	**4**
		8	**3**	**4**	**1**
			1	**1**	

B

	8	2	4		
6	**1**	**2**	**3**	3	
3	**3**	3	**1**	**2**	4
6	**4**	**2**	5 / 4	**1**	**3**
	4	**1**	**3**	1 / 1	**1**
		3	**2**	**1**	

A

2	3	3	4
1	1	2	3
3	2	3	1
4	1	4	2

B

4	3	2	1
1	1	4	2
2	4	3	4
1	4	2	2

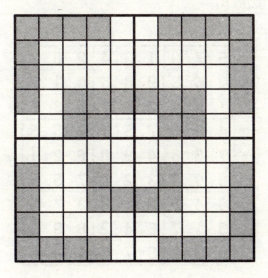

Puzzle 86

A Photography was introduced in the 1830s.

B The first films with sound were released in 1926.

C The name of the first public system for playing back films was the Kinetoscope.

D The Lumiére brothers demonstrated the first projector system in 1895.

Puzzle 87

5	7	9	1	3	4	2	6	8
2	6	3	9	8	5	4	1	7
1	8	4	2	6	7	5	3	9
4	2	6	7	5	1	9	8	3
7	3	5	4	9	8	6	2	1
8	9	1	3	2	6	7	5	4
6	4	8	5	1	9	3	7	2
3	1	7	6	4	2	8	9	5
9	5	2	8	7	3	1	4	6

A

2	•	1	1	3
1	•	•	•	3
1	•	•	2
2	2	3	3

B

3	2	2	3	3	3
3	2	1	2	1
3	1	1	1	3
2	2	1	1	2
3	2	3	3	3
2	2	2	1	2	2

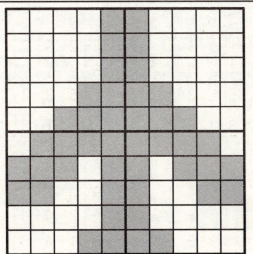

S	S	U	B	M	I	N	O	L	U	M	U	C	C
C	U	U	L	S	S	S	U	U	O	U	O	T	R
L	S	U	T	A	R	T	S	O	B	M	I	N	T
N	U	S	M	A	S	R	M	U	S	M	U	R	T
O	T	S	O	L	R	A	I	C	L	U	O	L	S
T	A	U	T	T	T	T	R	T	C	B	A	T	M
T	R	S	A	O	C	O	S	S	M	S	T	U	T
L	T	R	T	C	O	C	M	O	M	U	M	O	S
U	S	U	L	U	M	U	C	O	R	R	I	C	L
R	O	A	I	M	T	M	C	L	C	R	R	T	U
O	T	N	L	U	B	U	L	N	M	I	I	O	M
T	L	R	U	L	M	L	I	S	L	C	O	C	T
B	A	I	L	U	T	U	A	L	C	M	C	U	U
O	S	I	S	S	I	S	U	U	L	L	C	U	U

A

B

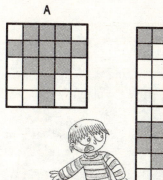

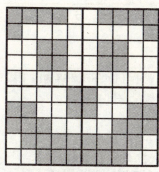

5	3	2	9	6	4	7	8	1
8	6	4	7	1	9	3	5	2
7	1	5	4	2	8	9	6	3
4	5	7	6	3	1	2	9	8
6	4	9	1	8	2	5	3	7
3	8	1	2	9	7	6	4	5
2	9	3	8	7	5	4	1	6
9	2	8	3	5	6	1	7	4
1	7	6	5	4	3	8	2	9

Code One
WELL DONE

Code Two
WHY DID THE COW WIN THE NOBEL PRIZE?

Code Three
BECAUSE IT WAS OUTSTANDING IN ITS FIELD!

A 49 clocks

B 6 clocks

C 13 clocks

D 29 clocks

E 6 clocks

F 18 different times

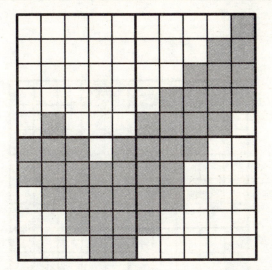

A   6 ways (1/6, 2/5, 3/4, 6/1, 5/2, 4/3)

B   The minimum total is 3
     The maximum total is 11

C   The minimum total is 7
     The maximum total is 11

D   2, 4, 6, 8, 10

E   3 doubles (1/1, 3/3, 5/5)

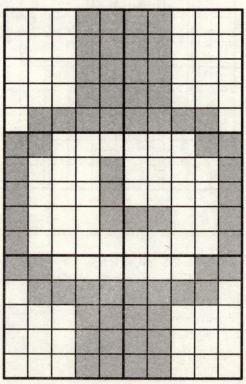

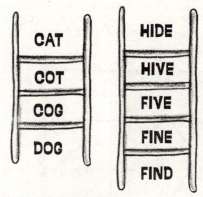

CAT
COT
COG
DOG

HIDE
HIVE
FIVE
FINE
FIND

Can you find any alternative solutions?

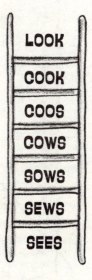

LOOK
COOK
COOS
COWS
SOWS
SEWS
SEES

3	9	5	2	8	6	7	4	1
1	2	6	4	5	7	3	9	8
7	4	8	1	3	9	6	5	2
2	6	4	8	7	3	9	1	5
9	3	1	5	4	2	8	7	6
5	8	7	6	9	1	2	3	4
4	7	2	3	1	8	5	6	9
6	5	3	9	2	4	1	8	7
8	1	9	7	6	5	4	2	3

	3	6		10	3	5
3	2	1	6	3	2	1
4	1	3	7 / 10	2	1	4
	7	2	1	4	6	
	4	3 / 6	3	1	2	3
7	1	2	4	4	3	1
6	3	1	2	3	1	2

The Puzzle Master

Dr Gareth Moore, who created all the puzzles in this book, is an ace puzzler, and author of lots of brain-training and puzzle books. He writes a monthly magazine called *Sudoku Xtra*, and runs an online puzzle site called PuzzleMix.com. Gareth got a PhD at the University of Cambridge, UK, where he taught machines to recognize the English language.